MAKING SWEETS

Written by Susannah Bradley

Illustrated by Cathy Hughes

HENDERSON
PUBLISHING LTD

©1991 HENDERSON PUBLISHING LTD

INTRODUCTION

How to use this book:

Sweetmaking is fun, but sometimes it can be dangerous. Boiling sugar is used to make toffee, and this reaches a very high temperature; so for this reason we have divided the recipes into the safe sort which you can make yourself, although if you need help don't be afraid to ask an adult, and those for which you must have adult help. And if that adult warns you to stand clear, DO SO!

Make sure that you have all the ingredients and utensils mentioned in the recipe you choose *before* you start to cook any of them; and thoroughly wash your hands at the start of each cooking session.

Have fun!

This book is divided into four sections:

Sweets you can make yourself

Sweets you can make with adult help

Sweets you can make in a microwave

Packaging your sweets for presents

LOVE HEARTS

Make something special for Valentine's Day!

1 size 3 egg	White icing bought in
300 g icing sugar	tube with piping
Red food colouring	nozzle

Utensils:
Tumbler
Saucer
Bowl
Heart-shaped biscuit cutter or pointed knife
Greaseproof paper
Fork or whisk
Rolling pin
Sieve

2. Whisk the egg white until frothy. Add the icing sugar, sieved. Add a few drops of red food colouring.

1. Break the egg into the saucer. Place the tumbler over the yolk and slide the white into the bowl. Save the yolk for cooking in something else, if needed.

3. Dust the working surface very lightly with icing sugar and roll out the fondant on it. Cut out heart shapes with the cutter.

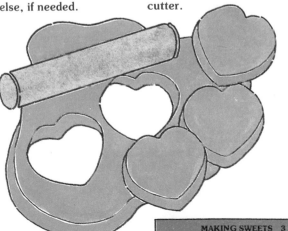

4. Gather together all the scraps, and roll out again. Cut out a few more.

5. Pipe words in white on each one like the message you get on bought sweets shaped like hearts. (Practise using the nozzle first, on greaseproof paper!)

6. Leave overnight in the fridge to set.

Suitable messages:
BE MINE ★ CHEAT! ★
I LOVE YOU ★
DARLING ★ YOU'RE
CUTE ★ LOVE ME ★
DON'T CRY ★
CALL ME ★ I'M SHY

SUGAR MICE

450 g icing sugar
1 size 3 egg
50 g golden syrup
2 teaspoons
cornflour

Silver balls
8 pieces of clean
string, each one
measuring 300 mm

Utensils:
Tumbler
Saucer
Whisk or fork
Wooden spoon
Mixing bowl
Polythene bag
Greaseproof paper

1. Break the egg on to the saucer. Put the tumbler over the yolk and tilt over the mixing bowl so that the white slides into it. You do not need the yolk for this recipe.

2. Lightly beat the white with the fork or whisk, until frothy. Add the golden syrup and half the egg white. Beat with the wooden spoon until smooth.

3. Add the rest of the sugar gradually, working it in bit by bit. When all of it has been used, dust the working surface with the cornflour and knead the mixture on it. When it is smooth and pliable break it up into eight equal portions. Put seven of them into the polythene bag to keep fresh while you work on the one remaining.

4. Pinch off a piece to form into ears and make the rest into a ball. Pull to a point one end for the nose and fix the ears on near this end. Push in two silver balls for eyes, and a string tail at the other end.

5. Make seven more and leave on greaseproof paper in a warm place to dry out for two days. Not in the fridge; they'll crack.

CHOCCY-YUM

1 Mars Bar
1 chocolate Flake

Utensils:
Heatproof bowl
Spoon
Plate
Saucepan
Sweet paper cases

3. Leave to cool for a while. When it is not too hot to handle, remove the bowl from the saucepan and form spoonfuls of the mixture into dice-sized cubes.

4. Put them on the plate to harden completely. When it is quite cool you can finish this off in the fridge.

1. Put some water in the saucepan and put it on the stove.

2. Cut the Mars and the Flake into small pieces and put them into the bowl. Put the bowl on top of the saucepan and heat until the chocolate is all melted.

SNOWBALLS

1 tablespoon orange juice	50 g raisins
25 g brown sugar	50 g dates
25 g desiccated coconut	50 g dried apricots, soaked overnight
	50 g ground almonds

Utensils:
Food processor or
liquidiser
Sweet paper cases

3. Put the desiccated coconut in a bowl and roll the balls in it until they are well coated.

1. Put the raisins, dates, apricots, ground almonds, orange juice and sugar in the food processor or liquidiser and whizz up into a paste.

2. Break off pieces and roll them into small balls.

4. Put them into their paper cases and chill them for 30 minutes before eating them.

COCONUT ICE

4 tablespoons condensed milk	175 g desiccated coconut
400 g icing sugar	Red food colouring

Utensils:
A sieve
A mixing bowl
Another bowl
A metal spoon
Spatula or flat-bladed kitchen knife
Baking tray

3. Put half the mixture into the other bowl and add a few drops of red food colouring, mixing it in well.

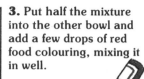

1. Sift the icing sugar through the sieve, using the metal spoon to rub through any lumps, into the mixing bowl.

4. Dust the baking tray with icing sugar and form each half of the mixture into a slab so that both slabs look identical. (Be careful — wash your hands thoroughly after handling the coloured half, or you will get colouring on the white portion, too.)

2. Mix in the condensed milk and the coconut. The mixture should be very stiff.

5. Press the two halves together on the dusted baking tray and leave to set firm.

RUM TRUFFLES

75 g plain chocolate
1 egg yolk
15 g butter
1 teaspoon whipped cream
1 teaspoon rum flavouring
Drinking chocolate
Chocolate vermicelli

Utensils:
Heatproof bowl
Saucepan small enough for the bowl to sit on so that the bottom of the bowl does not touch the bottom of the saucepan
Hand whisk or fork
Two teaspoons
2 shallow bowls
Plate

1. Put some water in the saucepan and heat it on the stove, with the heatproof bowl on top. Break the chocolate into small pieces and put them into the bowl to melt. When melted, remove bowl from heat.

2. Add the egg yolk, cream, butter and rum flavouring and stir. Beat together until thickened.

3. Put a little drinking chocolate powder into one bowl and some chocolate vermicelli in the other. Form pieces of the truffle mixture into small balls using the two teaspoons, and roll some in the drinking chocolate, some in the vermicelli, before putting them on a plate.

Rum truffle mixture
as given here
White fondant icing
Icing sugar

Small amount of
green coloured and
red coloured
marzipan

Utensils:
Pointed kitchen
knife
Cocktail stick
Plate
Teaspoon

3. Make tiny holly berries by rolling some red marzipan between your finger and thumb. Stick three holly berries in the top of each Christmas pud.

1. Make the truffles as already described in previous recipe.

2. Roll out the fondant icing on a surface dusted with icing sugar. Cut small uneven circles of it and place over the top half of each truffle to look like white sauce.

4. Make tiny green marzipan leaves using the knife, and mark a line down the centre of each with the cocktail stick. Push into place near the berries.

FROST-FRUIT

Grapes	Orange segments
Strawberries	An egg
Raspberries	Icing sugar

Utensils:
2 bowls
Saucer
Tumbler
Fork
Wire rack
A paintbrush

1. Separate the yolk from the white of the egg by cracking it into a saucer, placing a tumbler over the yolk, and tipping it so that the white drains into a bowl.

2. You don't need the yolk, but it may be used up with other eggs if anyone is making biscuits or scrambled egg.

3. Whisk the egg white with the fork until it is frothy.

4. Wash the fruit and let it drain on the wire rack.

5. Put some icing sugar into the other bowl.

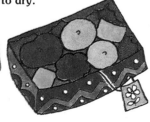

6. Paint each piece of fruit with egg white, roll it in the icing sugar, and place it on the wire rack to dry.

7. These are very nice with chocolate coated and marzipan fruits, if you want to give someone a really special box of delights.

PEPPERMINT CREAMS

1 size 3 egg
300 g icing sugar
Green food colouring

½ teaspoon
peppermint essence

Utensils:
Tumbler
Saucer
2 bowls
Small round cutter
Greaseproof paper
Rolling pin
Fork or whisk

1. Break the egg into a saucer. Place the tumbler over the yolk and slide the white into one of the bowls. Save the yolk for use in biscuits or scrambled egg, if anyone is making any.

2. Whisk the egg white with the fork or whisk. When it is frothy, sieve in the icing sugar a little at a time. Add the peppermint essence.

3. Knead until smooth, then dust your working surface with icing sugar and roll out half the mixture on it. Don't make it too thin and, if your rolling pin gets sticky, dust that with icing sugar, too.

4. Cut out circles of peppermint cream mixture and put on a plate. Do not overlap them. Gather up the scraps and roll them out again to make a few more.

6. Leave to dry out overnight in the fridge.

5. Add green colouring very sparingly to the other half of the mixture in the bowl. Roll this out and cut more peppermint creams from it, using the scraps as before.

JELLY GOLDFISH

1 packet of jelly
(orange)
300 ml boiling water

Utensils:
Metal spoon
Heatproof bowl
Shallow-sided
baking tray
Sharp knife

1. Break up the jelly and carefully pour the boiling water over it. Stir with the metal spoon until the jelly has melted.

2. Pour the jelly into the shallow tray and put it into the fridge to set.

3. Trace the goldfish pattern from this page and use it as a guide to cutting out goldfish from the set jelly.

4. Don't waste the scraps which are left over — chop and eat them in the traditional way, with ice cream.

MARZIPAN

There are many different ways of using marzipan to make sweets. You can buy it readymade or make your own.

The readymade sort can be bought in yellow or white, and you should buy white if possible, because it takes the clear food colours better.

Here is a recipe for you to make your own.

250 g icing sugar 250 g caster sugar 500 g ground almonds	1 tsp lemon juice Few drops vanilla essence Beaten egg to mix

Utensils:
A sieve
Mixing bowl
Clean working surface or slab which has been dusted with icing sugar
Metal spoon

2. Mix them all together, then add beaten egg in drips until you have enough to bind everything together — don't let it get too sloppy. Knead it between your fingers to make it smooth.

1. Sieve the icing sugar and caster sugar into the bowl, add the ground almonds, the lemon juice and the vanilla essence.

Marzipan (white, if possible)
Food colourings

Small amount icing sugar
A few cloves and sticks of angelica

Utensils:
Saucers, small bowls
or yogurt pots
Grater
Cocktail stick
Tweezers
Plate
Paintbrush

Tip: Dust your fingers with icing sugar to prevent stickiness and try to keep everything in proportion to other fruit and veg.

Oranges

Use orange food colouring, mixing together red and yellow if necessary. Work a little colouring at a time into enough marzipan for the amount of oranges you want to make — if you use too much the marzipan will go mushy. Make round balls and then roll each one over a grater to give it a pitted surface. Add a clove at one end if the 'orange' is big enough, and if it is not to be eaten by a small child (who might forget to take it out first).

Cherries

Cut a thin, V-shaped piece of liquorice bootlace for the stalks. Colour some marzipan red and make into smooth, shiny balls. Put them in pairs on each end of the stalk.

Apples

Apples come in a variety of colours so you can make green ones, or yellow ones with splashes of red painted on the side. They are not completely round like oranges — look at a real apple as you shape the marzipan. Use the cocktail stick to press the correct shape in top and bottom, and if you like, cut a stalk and a leaf out of angelica to fix in the top.

Strawberries

Make up some red marzipan and form into strawberry shapes — surely nobody needs to be told what that is! — and top with a spiky star-shaped piece of angelica (or you can use green marzipan if you prefer.) Use the cocktail sticks to make little marks where the pips would be.

Bananas

Make them long and curved, and pinch together two or three at the top to make a bunch. If you like you can paint on green bits for those which aren't quite ripe — or brown bits (mix together red and green food colouring) for those which are a little over-ripe!

Grapes

Cut a shred of liquorice bootlace for the stalk. Colour some marzipan green — or even purplish-black (using red, blue and a little green food colouring) and make tiny balls with it. Wedge them together in the shape of a bunch of grapes, around the liquorice stalk.

SWIMMING POOL CAKE

Packet of mint sticks
Sponge flan ring
Green jelly
Blue food colouring
Jelly babies

Rice paper
Square type of
liquorice allsorts
75 g chocolate

Utensils:
Heatproof bowl
Spoon
Knife
Large plate
Another heatproof
bowl
Saucepan
Yet another spoon

1. Make up the jelly according to the instructions on the packet. Add a drop or two of blue food colouring in to make it more the colour of swimming pool water. Leave in the fridge to set.

2. When it has set, chop it up finely. Place the flan ring on the plate and put enough jelly into it to fill it, but not too much so that it is piled up.

3. Cut the mint sticks all the same length, a little higher than the sides of the flan ring.

4. Melt the chocolate in a heatproof bowl over a saucepan of simmering water, and smear this all round the outside of the flan ring.

5. Fix the mint sticks into this like a fence, all the way round.

6. Make a diving board out of two mint stick pieces, side by side, placing them from the edge across the jelly at one point. Make an airbed to float on the water from two square liquorice allsort sweets, joined at the side with melted chocolate.

7. Make towels from pieces of rice paper, fringed at both ends and painted in stripes with food colouring.

8. Put jelly babies in for a swim, placing some in the choppy waters and others sunbathing on the sides, some on airbeds and others about to use the diving board.

9. This makes an interesting summer birthday cake, as long as the guests eat it at the party and don't try to take it home in a goody bag. You could have a rice paper banner stuck into it on a full-length mint stick, saying HAPPY BIRTHDAY, with the person's name on it.

FUDGE

500 g soft brown sugar
60 g margarine

275 ml milk
Vanilla essence

Utensils:
A heavy saucepan
A wooden spoon
A bowl of cold water
A baking tray with sides, 150 × 150 mm
A knife

1. Heat the butter, sugar, and milk in a saucepan over a gentle heat until the sugar has dissolved. It is best for a grown-up to do this part, because next you have to bring it to the boil, stirring all the time — and boil it for about 30 minutes.

2. Test to see if the fudge is ready by dropping a little from the stirring spoon into the bowl of cold water. If it is done, the drop will form itself into a small ball. If it doesn't, make your grown-up boil it for a bit longer and keep testing it until it does.

3. Take the mixture off the heat. Add a few drops of vanilla essence and beat it until creamy.

4. Pour it into the tin, leave it to set, and then cut it into squares.

CHOCOLATE FUDGE

150 ml milk	3 tablespoons cocoa
25 g margarine or butter	Pinch of salt
350 g sugar	1/2 teaspoon vanilla essence

Utensils:
Heavy saucepan
Wooden spoon
Whisk
Greased tin
Cup of cold water
Knife

1. Put all the ingredients except the vanilla in the saucepan and get a grown-up to look after it on the stove. First it has to be on a low light until the sugar has melted. Then it should be brought to the boil.

2. Continue to let it boil, gently, until the mixture can be formed into a small ball when some is dropped from the spoon into the cup of cold water.

3. Remove from the heat and let it cool slightly. Then add the vanilla and beat hard until it thickens.

4. Pour into the greased tin and mark in squares with the knife. Leave overnight until set.

TOFFEE

200 g granulated sugar
65 ml water

Pinch of cream of tartar

Utensils:
Heavy saucepan
Wooden spoon
Greased flat tin
Cup of cold water

1. Get a grown-up to do all the stove work because boiling toffee is dangerous stuff.

2. Heat everything together in the saucepan, stirring until the sugar is dissolved, over a low heat.

3. Once the sugar has dissolved, turn up the heat and boil without stirring until the toffee, now a brown colour, hardens and crackles when a little of it is dropped from the spoon into a cup of cold water.

4. Pour it into the greased tin and mark it into squares.

5. Leave it to set. Once it is cool you can put it into the fridge to finish hardening off. When that happens, take it out and break it up.

TOFFEE APPLES

Six eating apples Toffee recipe as before	Wooden lolly sticks Hundreds and thousands

Utensils:
As for Toffee recipe
Greased tray
Bowl

1. Wash and dry the apples. Push a lolly stick into each one near the core. Put the Hundreds and Thousands in the bowl.

3. Dip the toffee-coated apples into the bowl of Hundreds and Thousands before they are quite set. It doesn't make them taste better, but they look prettier.

2. Make the toffee. Remove it from the heat and dip the apples in it, holding them by their sticks. Twist them round to make sure they are coated.

4. Leave them on the greased tray.

TOFFEE-ORANGE TRIANGLES

Base:
175 g plain flour
¼ teaspoon ground cinnamon
125 g margarine
50 g caster sugar
Pinch of salt

Middle:
125 g margarine
125 g soft brown sugar
2 tablespoons golden syrup
150 ml condensed milk
1 tablespoon grated orange rind

Topping:
200 g plain chocolate

Utensils:
Heavy saucepan
Sieve
Mixing bowl
Wooden spoon
Greased 180 × 180 mm square tin, base-lined with greaseproof paper
Heatproof bowl
Knife
Whisk

1. Set the oven to Gas Mark 4, 350 F, 180 C.

2. Sieve the flour, salt and cinnamon into the mixing bowl. Rub in the margarine between your fingertips until the mixture looks like breadcrumbs.

3. Stir in the caster sugar. Spoon the mixture into the tin and press down firmly. Bake for 25 minutes, getting a grown-up to take it out at the end of that time. Leave until cold.

4. Make the filling by putting the butter, light brown sugar, golden syrup and condensed milk into the saucepan over a very low heat. Stir until everything has melted and simmer gently for seven minutes. Keep stirring!

6. When it is quite cold, add the topping by melting the chocolate in the heatproof basin over a pan of gently simmering water. Spread it in an even layer and leave until set.

5. Use the whisk to beat in the orange rind, being careful not to splash the hot mixture. Leave to cool for ten minutes, then pour the mixture over the base.

7. Cut into triangles.

CRISP TOFFEE SQUARES

Utensils:
180 mm square baking tin, greased
Large heatproof bowl
Saucepan
Wooden spoon
Fork
Knife

100 g margarine
100 g marshmallows
100 g plain toffees
100 g Rice Krispies

1. Half-fill the saucepan with water and place on the stove to heat. Place the large, heatproof bowl over this and into the bowl put the toffees, marshmallows and margarine. Ask a grown-up to stir it for you occasionally until all the ingredients in the pan have melted. Then ask the grown-up to take the bowl off the saucepan, and turn off the heat.

2. Let it cool a bit, then beat the mixture with the wooden spoon. Stir in the Rice Krispies, using the fork.

3. Spoon it all into the greased tin, pressing it down smoothly with the back of the spoon. Leave it to cool.

4. Let it harden overnight in the fridge and then cut it into squares.

MARSHMALLOWS

220 g granulated
sugar
265 ml hot water
1½ tablespoons
gelatine

½ teaspoon cream of
tartar
Vanilla flavouring
Icing sugar

Utensils:
Heavy saucepan
Wooden spoon
Bowl
Greased tin
Knife

1. Put all ingredients
except the vanilla into
the saucepan and get a
grown-up to heat it
gently until the sugar
has melted.

2. The mixture should
then be boiled for 2 to 3
minutes.

3. Pour it into the bowl
and leave to cool until a
skin is beginning to form
on the top.

4. Next, beat the
mixture with the wooden
spoon until it becomes
thick and white. Add the
vanilla.

5. Dust the greased tin
with icing sugar and
pour the mixture into it.
Leave overnight to set.

6. Next day, ease away
from the sides, turn out
on to some icing sugar,
and cut into cubes. Roll
them in icing sugar and
store in polythene bags,
well-secured to keep out
the air.

MUESLI CHEW BARS

Base:
280 g self-raising wholemeal flour

Middle:
340 g no-soak prunes

Topping:
170 g golden syrup
60 g margarine
230 g porridge oats
60 g sunflower seeds, grilled for 1 minute

230 g margarine
110 g light brown muscavado sugar

230 ml apple or orange juice

60 g unsalted peanuts, chopped and grilled for 1 minute
30 g sesame seeds, grilled for 1 minute

Utensils:
Liquidiser or food processor
Mixing bowl
Sieve
Fork
Knife
Wooden spoon
330 × 255 mm greased tin, lined with greaseproof paper on the base
Saucepan
Set the oven to Gas Mark 4, 350 F, 180 C.

1. Put the prunes and fruit juice in the saucepan and cook for ten minutes until tender. Put the mixture into the liquidiser or food processor to make the bits smaller. Wash up the saucepan.

2. Sift the flour into the mixing bowl (add the bran left in the sieve, too). Rub the fat in with your fingers until the mixture looks like breadcrumbs. Stir in the sugar.

3. Knead the mixture with your hands to bind it together, then press it into an even layer on the base of the tin. Prick all over with the fork and put it into the fridge for ten minutes. Then bake it for 15 minutes.

4. Get a grown-up to take it out of the oven for you as this can be dangerous. Leave it for five minutes before spreading the prune mixture over the top.

5. Get the saucepan out again! Melt the golden syrup in it over a low heat with the margarine. Stir in everything else and turn off the heat. Pile it evenly on top of the prunes and bake for around half an hour. Remember to get a grown-up to take it out of the oven again for you.

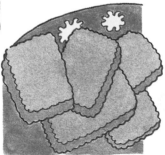

6. Leave to cool for about ten minutes, then mark it into 24 bars. Wait until it is quite cold before turning it out of the tray.

7. Store it in an airtight tin for up to five days, or in a freezer for a month.

CRYSTALLISED PINEAPPLE

| 1 fresh pineapple | 250 ml water |
| 450 g granulated sugar | 200 g caster sugar |

Utensils:
Strong, sharp knife
Chopping board
Heavy saucepan
Slotted spoon
Brown paper
Bowl
Baking trays

1. Cut the top and base from the pineapple and throw them away. Cut off the skin, and also the spines which run round the pineapple in rows. This should be done by a grown-up, in case you cut yourself.

2. Chop the remaining pineapple flesh into chunks and put on one side.

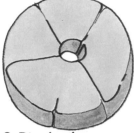

3. Dissolve the granulated sugar in the saucepan with the water over a low heat. Bring the liquid to the boil. Add the pineapple and gently boil for an hour, keeping an eye on it all the time to make sure that it doesn't boil over.

4. Take out the pineapple pieces with the slotted spoon, draining off as much liquid as possible.

5. Put the caster sugar in the bowl and roll the pineapple pieces in it. Spread brown paper on to the baking trays and spread the pineapple pieces on it. Dry them in a cool oven, on the lowest setting you can, for two hours, then take them out and roll them again in caster sugar. Store in an airtight jar.

TURKISH DELIGHT

300 ml water
25 g powdered gelatine
450 g granulated sugar
1/2 level teaspoon citric acid
50 g icing sugar

Red food colouring — and rosewater, if you can get it
1/2 level teaspoon bicarbonate of soda
Another 1/2 level teaspoon citric acid
Cooking oil

Utensils:
A heavy saucepan
Wooden spoon
A sieve
A cake tin measuring 180 × 180 × 25 mm
A polythene bag
Greaseproof paper
A large bowl
A long, sharp knife
An airtight tin

Note: It takes two days to make Turkish Delight. (If you have a microwave, use our other recipe.)

1. Put the water in the saucepan and sprinkle the gelatine on to it. Stir it in. Let it soak for ten minutes.

2. Put the saucepan over a gentle heat and stir until the gelatine has dissolved. When the liquid is clear, add one measure of citric acid and the sugar and stir until this dissolves, too. Don't splash the sides of the saucepan or the Turkish Delight could end up lumpy.

3. Turn the heat up and bring the mixture to the boil. Boil it for 20 minutes without stirring.

4. When the mixture is the colour of pale straw take the pan off the heat. When it has stopped frothing, skim the scum from the top with your spoon. Leave it to cool for 25 minutes or until thick, cool and nearly solid. Add a few drops of red food colouring and rosewater.

5. Grease the cake tin with the oil and put some greaseproof paper in the base. Oil this, too. Carefully pour in the mixture and leave in the fridge to set; leave it overnight!

6. Sieve together the icing sugar, bicarbonate of soda and the other measure of citric acid. Mix them together and leave the mixed powders in the polythene bag for the next day.

7. Next day, sprinkle half the mixed powders on to a sheet of greaseproof paper. Put the rest into the large bowl.

8. Loosen the sides of the Turkish Delight with the knife, then turn it upside down so that it falls on to the powdered greaseproof paper. Peel off the lining paper, then turn the slab of Turkish Delight over again to coat the other side with the powder.

9. Run the knife under the tap and cut the Turkish Delight into squares. Place them in the bowl and shake them to make sure they are covered.

10. Line the airtight tin with greaseproof paper and store whatever is left from the first nibbles you take of it!

Many of the sweets in this book can be made in the microwave if a grown-up helps you to adapt the times and utensils — here are some with special microwave instructions.

225 g toffees
50 g butter
1 tablespoon double cream
150 g icing sugar

100 g salted peanuts
75 g hazelnuts
100 g desiccated coconut
Red food colouring

Utensils:
Shallow dish suitable for the microwave
Sieve
Spoon
Greaseproof paper

2. Cook on Medium power for 5 minutes, or until the toffees have melted, stirring twice during this time.

1. Unwrap the toffees and put them into the dish with the butter.

3. Stir in the cream. Sift the icing sugar over it and beat it in.

4. Stir in the nuts.

5. Leave to cool for twenty minutes.

6. Add a drop of food colouring to the coconut to turn it pink, using your hands to rub it in.

7. Shape the toffee mixture, when cool enough, into little oblong shapes and roll in the coconut. Place them on greaseproof paper and put them in the fridge to harden.

RASPBERRY CONES

Plain chocolate
Raspberry jam
Fresh raspberries

Utensils:
Greaseproof paper
Scissors
Microwave-proof
bowl
Sticky tape
Saucer
Pencil
Spoon

3. Cut out the circle of greaseproof paper.

4. Cut the circle into quarters. Take one quarter and fold it into a cone shape, securing it with sticky tape. Be careful not to get any sticky tape on the inside.

1. The following instructions tell you how to make one of these cones. Make as many as you have ingredients for.

2. Draw with the pencil round a saucer which is upside down on the greaseproof paper.

5. Melt the chocolate in the bowl in the microwave. Use the spoon to coat the inside of the cone. Try to coat it evenly.

6. Leave in the fridge for an hour until set really firmly.

8. Spoon a little melted chocolate on top of the jam. Press some raspberries into this.

7. Put a spoonful of jam into the cone.

9. Remove the paper. Chill until you are ready to serve.

TURKISH DELIGHT

25 g gelatine
450 g granulated
sugar
1/2 teaspoon citric
acid
50 g icing sugar

2 drops red food
colouring
1 tablespoon
rosewater
1/2 teaspoon
bicarbonate of soda

Utensils:
Large microwave-
proof bowl
190 mm square
metal cake tin,
well-greased
with oil
Spoon
Sieve
Cup
Greaseproof paper
Knife

2. Put the sugar and half
the citric acid into the
large bowl and mix
thoroughly. Stir in the
gelatine. Cook on Full
power for 6 minutes.

1. Sprinkle the gelatine
(we used two and a bit
sachets to make up the
25 g) into 250 ml water
and cook it on Full
power for 1 minute.

3. Stir in the rosewater
and the food colouring,
and leave to cool for 25
minutes.

4. Pour the mixture into the greased tin and pop it into the fridge overnight.

5. Next day, mix up the other ¼ teaspoonful of citric acid with the icing sugar and bicarbonate of soda. Spread some of this on a sheet of greaseproof paper.

6. Gently ease the Turkish Delight away from the side of the tin and with *very* clean fingers pull it up from the base. Turn it out on to the sherberty greaseproof paper and cut into squares with the knife.

7. Toss the squares in the rest of the sherbert. If you can't manage to eat it all at once, store it in an airtight container, with the sherbert around it.

HONEYCOMB TOFFEE

225 g granulated
sugar
1 tablespoon white
wine vinegar
150 ml boiling water

¼ teaspoon vanilla
essence
½ teaspoon
bicarbonate of soda
Oil

Utensils:
150 mm square cake
tin (metal)
Large microwave-
proof bowl
Spoon
Bowl of cold water

1. Grease the cake tin
well inside with oil.
Put the sugar, boiling
water, vinegar and
vanilla essence into the
microwave-proof bowl
and cook in the
microwave on full power
for 12 minutes. Stir twice
during this time. Keep
an eye on it because it
should not turn brown
but should be the colour
of honey so if it seems to
be turning brown, stop
the cooking process and
test it.

2. To test to see if it is
done, drop a little of the
syrup from the spoon
into the bowl of cold
water. If done, it will
lengthen into a strand,
which breaks easily.

3. Cook for a further
minute if this does not
happen, and again if
necessary.

4. Take the syrup from the microwave and sprinkle the bicarbonate of soda into it. Very quickly stir it until it froths up, then pour it immediately into the greased tin. You have to be very quick to do this. Don't stir it once it reaches the tin but tilt the tin so that the corners get their share of mixture.

5. Let it harden somewhere cool — then bash it into small pieces to eat.

CHOCOLATE CHERRIES

Melting chocolate in the microwave is easy if you don't overdo it. The amount of time it takes depends on how much chocolate you are trying to melt. The best way is to give it one minute at a time and let the heat of the already melted bits melt any lumps which remain, rather than put it back to melt the lumps and risk burning the melted parts.

> Glacé cherries
> Plain chocolate

> Utensils:
> Cocktail sticks
> Microwave-proof bowl
> Cheese grater (the curved sort) or something else into which you could stick cocktail sticks to prop them up

1. Melt the chocolate in the microwave. Spear each cherry with a cocktail stick and dip it until coated in the chocolate.

2. Stick the cocktail stick into a hole in the grater and leave until set.

3. If you haven't got the right sort of grater, you could cut an orange in half and place cut side down so that you could use the domed peel for sticking in your cocktail sticks.

4. Remove the cocktail sticks when the chocolate has set. You could use this method for covering pineapple chunks, or for dipping the points of strawberries, which looks lovely when the red of the fruit peeps over the chocolate part.

Sesame seeds	**Sunflower seeds**
Plain chocolate	**Salted peanuts**

Utensils:
Food processor, or a grown-up willing to chop things up for you
Microwave-proof bowl
Paper sweet cases
Mixing spoon
Teaspoon

2. Melt the chocolate in the microwave-proof bowl.

3. Put the nuts and seeds into the melted chocolate and mix them all up together until coated. Put spoonsful of the mixture into the paper sweet cases and leave in a cool place until set.

1. Chop up the seeds and peanuts together in the food processor, or get a grown-up to do it by hand. Don't try to do it yourself as it can be dangerous; if you haven't got a food processor or a grown-up, try crushing the peanuts in a polythene bag with a rolling pin, and leave the sunflower seeds whole.

SWEETS AS PRESENTS

You may have noticed, as you look through this book, that many of the recipes say: Chill in the fridge before eating. This is impossible to do when you are giving them as a present, unless you happen to be standing next to the fridge at the time. But you should tell the peson who is getting the present that they will taste better if they are chilled first. Then leave it up to them; some people just like to gobble them up without bothering if they are chilled or not!

Make up several different sorts for a special selection, and try to vary them, so that there are nutty ones next to jellies, chocolates as well as peppermint creams. Packaging is very important, so save any bows, nice boxes, paper doilies and so on which come your way. If you haven't got any of these things don't go out and spend a lot of money on wrappings; silver foil covering an ordinary carton turned on its side and slit sideways can look special too.

Open out a box to see how it is made, and make a pattern from it. Or cover the box itself, and stick your own label on the outside. On the next few pages we give you some packaging ideas to try out.

This is no good for the sort of sweets which stick to each other, but anything you can wrap up will do to fill it.

Pencil
Kitchen roll middle
Wrapping paper
Glue
Scissors
Small piece of card
Small piece of narrow ribbon
Brass paper fastener
Sweets small enough to slide up and down the tube.

1. Place the kitchen roll middle on end on the wrong side of the wrapping paper and draw round it.

2. Leaving an overlap, cut it out. Make another one the same.

3. Snip in from the outer edge at small intervals all round, as far as the pencil line.

4. Cut out another circle of wrapping paper and two of card, but for these don't leave any overlap on them — cut around the pencil line instead.

5. Glue one piece of card to the wrong side of one of the larger paper circles which has been snipped.

6. Put it to the bottom of the kitchen roll middle. Fold up and glue the tabs to the kitchen roll middle to hold the base in place.

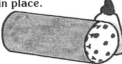

7. Glue the remaining cardboard circle to the wrong side of the larger, snipped, paper circle. Fold the snipped edges to the other side and glue down.

8. Glue the ribbon in position as shown on the tabbed side of this circle.

9. Glue the small circle of paper remaining over the ribbon on the cardboard circle.

10. Glue the cut end of the ribbon to the top of the tube so that it sits on top like a lid.

11. Cover the tube with wrapping paper, neatly covering up all the bottom tabs and the ribbon ends. Try to get the join at the back.

12. Make a hole with the point of the scissors at the front, where the loop of ribbon falls. Push the brass paper fastener through and fix in place.

13. Put the sweets inside, loop the ribbon round the paper fastener — and give it away!

CHRISTMAS TREE CONES

Full of sweets, these little cones will look cute on the Christmas tree. Make them in red and green shiny paper, and have plenty of sweets standing by to pop into them when they mysteriously keep emptying!

Piece of shiny
wrapping paper
Thin card, 400 mm
square
Glue
Red ribbon
Glitter

1. Cover both sides of card with shiny paper.

2. Fold into a cone shape, overlapping slightly.

3. Glue front edges together.

4. Make a small hole in the top corner and thread the ribbon through. Tie a knot in it, and hang it on the tree.

5. Fill it with sweets.

6. These cones can be made at other times of the year, too. Try making them in stiff coloured paper, and peg them to a line strung across the room. You could cut out the letters in HAPPY BIRTHDAY and put one on each cone like a banner. Then everyone can have one to take home afterwards.

**Last Word:
NOW GO AND CLEAN YOUR TEETH!**